This is my *letter*
to the *World*
That never wrote
to *Me*—
The simple *News*
that Nature told —
With tender *Majesty*

Her *Message* is committed
To Hands I cannot see —
For *love* of Her —
Sweet — countrymen —
Judge tenderly
—of *Me*

This is my letter to the World
That never wrote to Me —
The simple News that Nature told —
With tender Majesty

Her Message is committed
To Hands I cannot see —
For love of Her — Sweet — countrymen —
Judge tenderly — of Me

VISIONS IN POETRY

EMILY DICKINSON

My letter TO THE *World*

AND OTHER POEMS

WITH ILLUSTRATIONS BY
ISABELLE ARSENAULT

KCP POETRY
An Imprint of Kids Can Press

There's a certain Slant of light,
   Winter Afternoons —
That oppresses, like the Heft
   Of Cathedral Tunes —

Heavenly Hurt, it gives us —
   We can find no scar,
But internal difference,
   Where the Meanings, are —

None may teach it — Any —
   'Tis the Seal despair —
An imperial affliction
   Sent us of the Air —

When it comes,
  the Landscape listens —
Shadows — hold their breath —

When it goes 'tis like the Distance
On the look of Death —

Because I could not stop for Death —
He kindly stopped for me —
The Carriage held but just Ourselves —
And Immortality.

We slowly drove —
    He knew no haste
And I had put away
    My labor and my leisure too,
For His Civility —

We passed the School,
   where Children strove
   At Recess — in the Ring —
We passed the Fields of Gazing Grain —
   We passed the Setting Sun —

Or rather — He passed Us —
   The Dews drew quivering and chill —
For only Gossamer, my Gown —
   My Tippet — only Tulle —

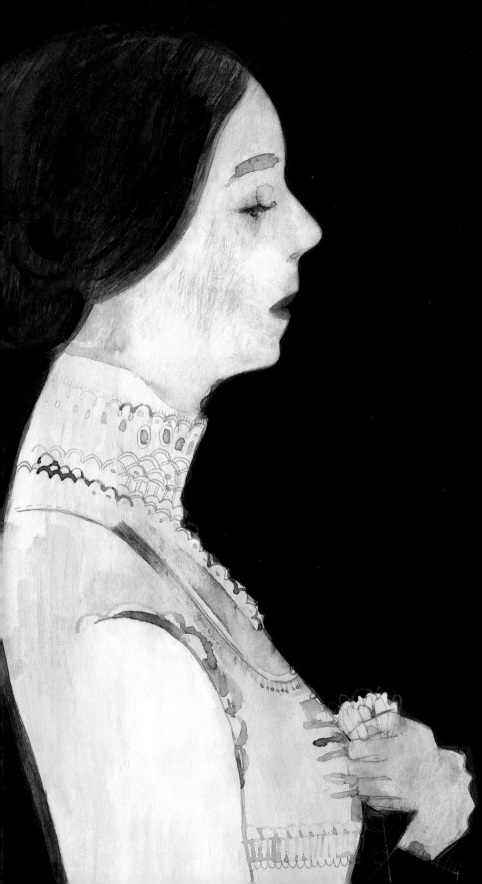

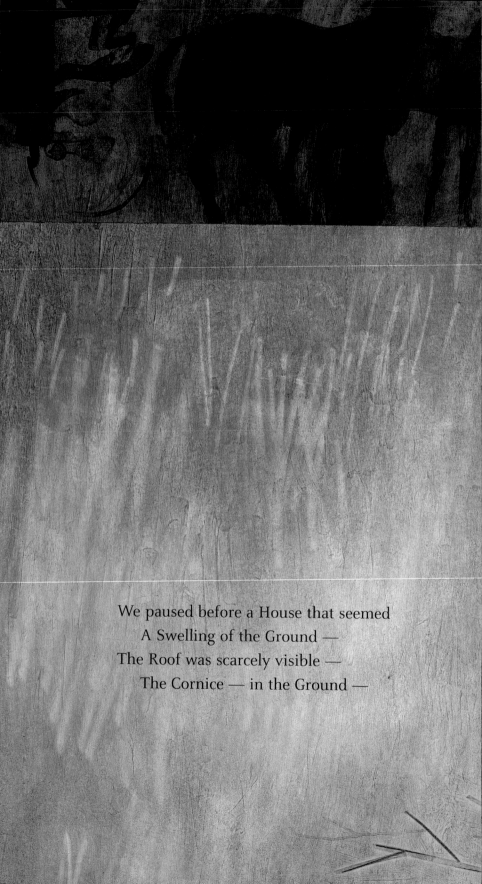

We paused before a House that seemed
A Swelling of the Ground —
The Roof was scarcely visible —
The Cornice — in the Ground —

Since then — 'tis Centuries — and yet
　　Feels shorter than the Day
I first surmised the Horses' Heads
　　Were toward Eternity —

I'm Nobody! Who are you?
Are you — Nobody — Too?
Then there's a pair of us!
Don't tell! they'd advertise
— you know!

How dreary — to be — Somebody!
How public — like a Frog —
To tell one's name — the livelong June —
To an admiring Bog!

I felt a Funeral, in my Brain,
    And Mourners to and fro
Kept treading — treading —
    till it seemed
That Sense was breaking through —

And when they all were seated,
  A Service, like a Drum —
Kept beating — beating — till I thought
  My Mind was going numb —

And then I heard them lift a Box
And creak across my Soul
With those same Boots of Lead, again,
Then Space — began to toll,

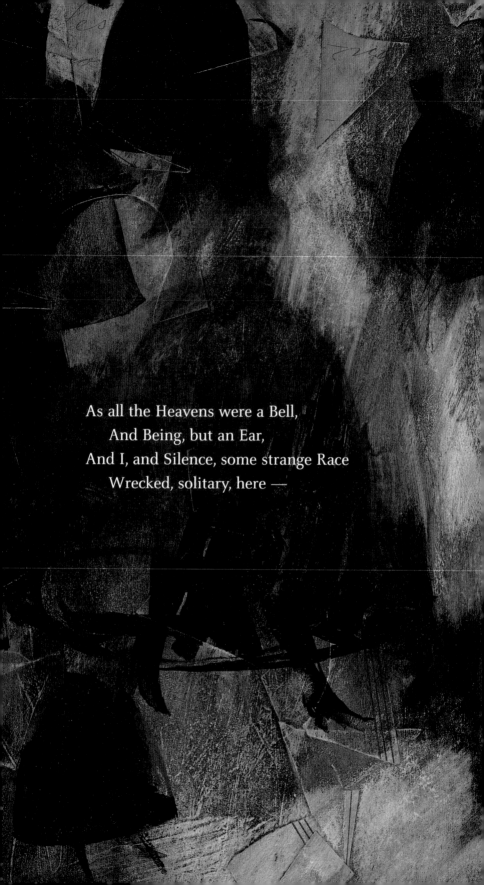

As all the Heavens were a Bell,
  And Being, but an Ear,
And I, and Silence, some strange Race
  Wrecked, solitary, here —

And then a Plank
   in Reason, broke,
And I dropped down,
   and down —

And hit a World,
   at every plunge,
And Finished
   knowing — then —

I cannot live with You —
    It would be Life —
And Life is over there —
    Behind the Shelf —

The Sexton keeps the Key to
    Putting up
Our Life — His Porcelain —
    Like a Cup —

Discarded of the Housewife —
    Quaint — or Broke —
A newer Sevres pleases —
    Old Ones crack —

I could not die — with You —
    For One must wait
To shut the Other's Gaze down —
    You — could not —

And I — Could I stand by
    And see You — freeze —
Without my Right of Frost —
    Death's privilege?

Nor could I rise — with You —
    Because Your Face
Would put out Jesus' —
    That New Grace

Grow plain — and foreign
    On my homesick Eye —
Except that You than He
    Shone closer by —

They'd judge Us — How —
    For You — served Heaven —
    You know,
Or sought to —
    I could not —

Because You saturated Sight —
    And I had no more Eyes
For sordid excellence
    As Paradise

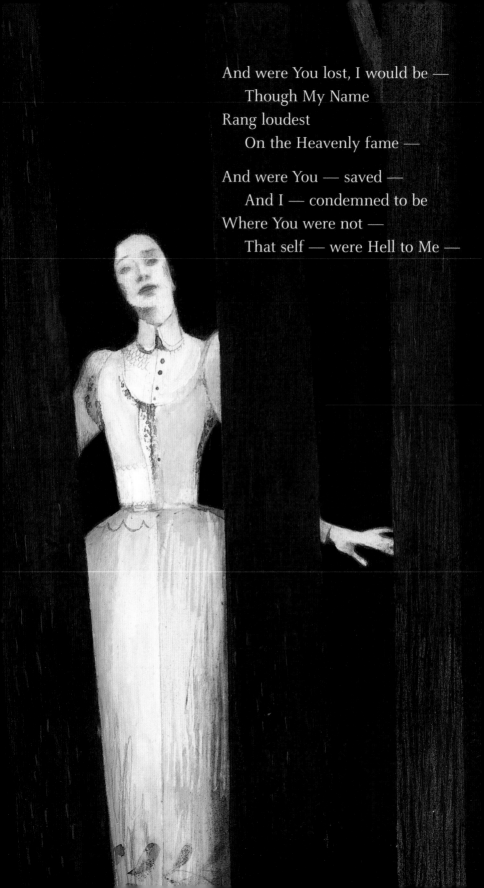

And were You lost, I would be —
    Though My Name
Rang loudest
    On the Heavenly fame —

And were You — saved —
    And I — condemned to be
Where You were not —
    That self — were Hell to Me —

So We must meet apart —
    You there — I — here —
With just the Door ajar
    That Oceans are — and Prayer —
And that White Sustenance —
    Despair —

"*Hope*" is the thing with feathers —
That perches in the soul —
And sings the tune without the words —
And never stops — at all —

And sweetest — in the Gale — is heard —
And sore must be the storm —
That could abash the little Bird
That kept so many warm —

I've heard it in the chillest land —
    And on the strangest Sea —
Yet, never, in Extremity,
    It asked a crumb — of Me.

Emily Dickinson

American poet Emily Dickinson (1830–1886) is one of the most legendary figures in literature, renowned for her personal eccentricities as much as for her poetry. A diminutive, childlike woman who never married and clad herself in white, Dickinson led an increasingly introverted and reclusive existence until her death in her father's house, the very house she was born in and had rarely left over the years. In fact, in the latter part of her life, Dickinson confined herself almost entirely to her room. She avoided face-to-face interactions, communicating instead with a chosen few mainly by means of correspondence — flurries of cryptic notes and letters that included fragments of verse. Even as a poet, Dickinson maintained her privacy: although a prolific writer, during her lifetime she consented to publish anonymously only a handful of her poems. It wasn't until after her death that a cache of almost eighteen hundred poems was discovered by her sister, Lavinia, and published in 1890.

Dickinson's unconventionality extended to her writing. Her use of short lines, slant rhyme, irregular punctuation and capitalization, startling vocabulary and imagery and her penchant for untitled verse did not conform to nineteenth-century ideals of poetry. Notable for their wit, wordplay and elliptical language, Dickinson's poems have a verbal density and richness that their seemingly simple surfaces belie. Yet despite the sometimes difficult and inscrutable quality of her verse and her tendency to morbid subject matter, few poets enjoy such widespread popularity as Emily Dickinson. The seven poems in this collection are not only some of her most famous works, they are some of the most celebrated poems of the last two centuries. It's ironic that she who shrank so much from the world, famously declaring, "I'm Nobody! Who are you?", became a beloved Somebody. Perhaps the reason for this universal fondness for, and fascination with, Emily is that her poems speak to us intimately, profoundly and with a modern sensibility about experiences, thoughts and feelings that resonates with us all, as if they were indeed precious letters from a close friend. There can be no doubt that Dickinson's "letters to the world" are among the most treasured lines in the English language.

Isabelle Arsenault

Isabelle Arsenault's rich and sensitive interpretation of seven of Emily Dickinson's greatest poems is a rare window into the life and soul of this enigmatic poet. Clever biographical details woven throughout these poignant, haunting illustrations subtly reveal aspects of Dickinson's character and daily existence, such as her self-imposed isolation, her obsessive writing, her deeply felt connection to nature and her preoccupation with death. Indeed, Arsenault links the poems visually with repeating motifs of houses, domestic objects, coffins and graves, flowers, birds and trees, paper scraps, pen and ink and by featuring Dickinson herself, in her ghostly white dress, in all of them. The illustrations also vividly evoke Emily's inner world, the subject matter of almost all her work. As the opening image suggests, Dickinson's "letters" take root and blossom into the surreal, dreamlike visions that follow — visions of death, despair, immortality, love, madness and, ultimately, hope and the power of creativity.

Arsenault's spare yet sophisticated and expressive style together with her thought-provoking imagery perfectly capture the essence of Dickinson's poetry. The twin-towered cathedral and ominous shadow in "There's a certain Slant of light," eerily suggestive of the events of 9/11; the grave-cum-house in "Because I could not stop for Death"; the dislocated treading feet in "I felt a Funeral, in my Brain"; the lover as a cracked teacup in "I cannot live with You" and the quill-pen and ink landscape of "'Hope' is the thing with feathers" — all are images that are as unique, surprising and captivating as the verses that conjured them. Arsenault's brilliant illustrations enable Emily's words to speak to the souls of a whole new generation — and they will make those already familiar with her work hear her as if for the very first time.

Isabelle Arsenault's editorial illustrations grace the pages of many newspapers and magazines throughout North America. She is also gaining a reputation as one of Canada's premier children's book illustrators. *Le coeur de monsieur Gaugin*, her first book for young people, earned her the Governor General's Award for Illustration, the country's most prestigious literary prize. Arsenault lives in Montreal, Quebec, with her husband and their two sons.

For my mom, my mother-in-law and my precious friend
Martine, who generously took care of little Florent
while I was away, playing with Emily — I.A.

The illustrations for this book were rendered in mixed media.

The text was set in
Celeste and *Dear Sarah*

KCP Poetry is an imprint of Kids Can Press

Kids Can Press acknowledges the financial support of the Government of
Ontario, through the Ontario Media Development Corporation's Ontario Book
Initiative; the Ontario Arts Council; the Canada Council for the Arts; and
the Government of Canada, through the BPIDP, for our publishing activity.

Published in Canada by   Published in the U.S. by
Kids Can Press Ltd.   Kids Can Press Ltd.
29 Birch Avenue   2250 Military Road
Toronto, ON M4V 1E2   Tonawanda, NY 14150

www.kidscanpress.com

Edited by Tara Walker
Designed by Karen Powers
Printed and bound in China

The hardcover edition of this book is smyth sewn casebound.
The paperback edition of this book is limp sewn with a drawn-on cover.

CM 08 0 9 8 7 6 5 4 3 2 1
CM PA 08 0 9 8 7 6 5 4 3 2 1

Library and Archives Canada Cataloguing in Publication

Dickinson, Emily, 1830–1886.
My letter to the world and other poems / Emily Dickinson ;
illustrations by Isabelle Arsenault.

(Visions in Poetry)
ISBN 978-1-55453-103-5 (bound). ISBN 978-1-55453-339-8 (pbk.)

I. Arsenault, Isabelle, 1978– II. Title.

PS1541.A6 2008   j811'.4   C2007-907040-X

Kids Can Press is a ʦℴℛℐℐS™ Entertainment company